I BELIEVE

I Can Find Solutions to Any Challenge or Adversity, Just Like Max, the Cat.

Coloring and Activity Book 8

SUZANNE MONDOUX
Illustrated by Gaëtanne Mondoux

BALBOA
PRESS
A DIVISION OF HAY HOUSE

Balboa Press books may be ordered through booksellers or by contacting:

Balboa Press
A Division of Hay House
1663 Liberty Drive
Bloomington, IN 47403
www.balboapress.com
1 (877) 407-4847

Because of the dynamic nature of the Internet, any web addresses or links contained in this book may have changed since publication and may no longer be valid. The views expressed in this work are solely those of the author and do not necessarily reflect the views of the publisher, and the publisher hereby disclaims any responsibility for them.

The author of this book does not dispense medical advice or prescribe the use of any technique as a form of treatment for physical, emotional, or medical problems without the advice of a physician, either directly or indirectly. The intent of the author is only to offer information of a general nature to help you in your quest for emotional and spiritual well-being. In the event you use any of the information in this book for yourself, which is your constitutional right, the author and the publisher assume no responsibility for your actions.

Any people depicted in stock imagery provided by Getty Images are models, and such images are being used for illustrative purposes only. Certain stock imagery © Getty Images.

Print information available on the last page.

ISBN: 978-1-9822-2273-4 (sc)
ISBN: 978-1-9822-2274-1 (e)

Balboa Press rev. date: 02/22/2019

This book belongs to

_____

I am _____ years old

Spring arrived on the ranch. The wet mushy snow turned to puddles for the children and animals to jump in and out of. The buds on the tree branches got bigger and bigger until green leaves popped out of them. And little yellow and red flowers began to sprout out of the ground. The sun was a little higher in the sky and a little warmer.

One evening when everyone was sitting around the campfire, Jojo announced a visitor would be arriving in the morning. She asked Teddy and Carlo to share their story of how they came to know Sara, the gold horse with the beautiful silver mane.

The girls and boys sat up straight on their logs in anticipation. Julie always loved having stories told to her. Sam sat closer to Carlo and Teddy. He wanted to hear every word. Paul opened his little notebook waiting to draw the scenes as they were recited. And Suzie curled up with Rocky as they played music quietly in the background. They wanted to pretend they were writing the music for a movie that was about to be told to them in detail.

Once everyone was settled Carlo and Teddy described the day they met Sara in the desert with the other Mustang horses. They talked about how Sara taught them to draw and paint. How they learned to become better artists through laugh and play, and lots of practice. They applied themselves to their craft every day. And most importantly they believed in themselves. They believed they could learn.

"Sara had come from a cruel place before she found the Mustang horses in the desert," said Carlo. "Her body and her heart bear the scars of that experience. Her fear of many people and many situations remained with her for many years. With the help of her new friends and learning to become an artist, she began to know herself, trust herself, believe in herself and trust and believe in others as well. She came to know what it felt like to have others be kind to her and love her. This allowed her to be kind and love others as well."

Carlo showed some of their paintings. They were of the places they had been. One particular painting was a painting of the ranch in the winter. "This was the first snow fall last year," said Carlo. Everyone examined the painting.

"You capture the finest of details," said Jojo.

From the corner of his eye Teddy spotted something in the bushes. He waited a moment before bringing attention to the rustling of the leaves.

"What else can you tell us about Sara?" asked Jojo.

Carlo and Teddy's dramatic and colorful account of their time spent with Sara illustrated the importance of believing in yourself. That everyone can learn when others believe in you. But most importantly when you believe in yourself. From her own story they had shown how she had occupied her mind with what she could do instead of what she could not, and she occupied her mind with what she believed about herself and not what others said about her, that was not true. She found the courage to overcome her cruel history by being true to herself, remaining authentic and kind and loving with herself.

The rustling in the bushes grew louder and louder. Everyone turned towards the noise. "What is that?" said Rocky.

Before anyone could answer an orange tabby cat crawled out from beneath the bushes. He looked up at everyone.

Jojo walked towards the cat. She lowered her head and nudged her nose against the cat. "Welcome. Come join us next to the fire."

The cat was covered in scars, the bones were protruding from the skin with each stride, and one eye was shut.

Everyone stared at the cat. They had never seen a cat like that before. It just happened fish soup had been served for dinner that night. Julie ran to the kitchen and came back with a warm bowl of fish soup. She placed it next to the cat. The cat licked the bowl clean.

"Now that you've had your dinner," said Jojo. "Can you tell us your name?" She nudged her leg against the cat and pushed up closer to the fire. The cat sat next to Julie.

"Thank you for the fish soup," said the cat. "My name is Max."

"Welcome Max," said everyone. "Welcome Max," said Julie. She patted Max on the head.

"Where do you come from?" said Teddy.

"I don't know," answered Max. "I have been walking for days and days through the forest, the valley and down those mountains."

"Can you describe where you were before you started walking and arrived here at our ranch?" said Carlo.

"I will try," said Max. "I remember there was lots of rain. The wind was blowing. Many things were flying around and crashing into each other. The water from the sea rushed into our yard. My family was scrambling around in the house trying to stop the water from coming into the house. All the neighbors gathered around helping each other. They were all trying to stop the water from rushing into their houses. But the water was coming into our yards very fast. Everyone got into their cars and drove as far away as they could. Many got stuck because the water rose too high and they could not drive their cars through the water."

Julie put her arm around Max. He tucked his head against her leg.

"Where were you when this was going on?" said Jojo.

Max wiped his tears. "I was hiding high up in the tree. The water rose half way up the tree. There was nowhere I could jump and reach my family. They called and called my name but I was too terrified to jump into the water. The water crushed everything it touched. The wind blew all night. I hung on as tight as I could in the tree. Then I fell asleep. When I woke up the sun was shining bright. It was very calm all around me. But no one was around. My family was gone. The water had receded enough for me to jump onto the roof of the house. That was the day I started walking. I jumped from roof to roof looking for my family. But I never found them. I have been looking ever since."

Max licked the wound on his foot.

"You are very brave," said Rocky. "You have come a long way, you have encountered many obstacles, and you overcame everyone. Yes, you appear as though you have had some challenges but your wounds will heal."

Max pointed at his closed eye. "I tumbled down a rocky slope. But I got back up on my feet, and that is when I cut the pad on my paw."

Jojo examined his wounds. "We will look after you. By morning you will feel much better. You are welcome to stay with us as long as you desire. In a week or so you will feel stronger and will have put on a bit of weight. Then you are welcome to join us in our daily lessons. We do many things here."

Max relaxed his tail and coiled it around his body. "I would like to find my family," said Max.

"Of course, we will help you with that as well. But first we will get you well to travel again," said Jojo.

"I heard you speak of Sara. I would like to meet her tomorrow when she arrives. Can I meet her as well?" said Max.

Carlo brought out the portrait he had done of Sara. "This is her," said Carlo. "Like her you have overcome a great challenge. You did not give up in the face of adversity. You will have much to discuss with Sara."

Max walked closer to the portrait. He looked at Sara with curious eyes. With his paw he touched the spot where Sara bore a scar on her flank.

The fire was slowly dwindling into ashes. Mouths were opened wide followed by yawns. It was time for bed. Max spent the night curled up next to Jojo.

By the time everyone woke up Sara had been visiting with Carlo and Teddy at the breakfast table. When Max joined them for breakfast, Sara knew everything there was needed to know about Max.

After breakfast Sara invited Max to join her for a walk in the field. They spent the day talking about their adventures and how they conquered every challenge they came across. They had become an inspiration for each other. They described what they would like to achieve in the near future and later in life as well. This talk served them both as a clear guide for choosing current and future courses of action.

Sara realized she was also on a new journey. She had left the desert to come help Jojo at the ranch. Through her trials and tribulation and her life with the Mustangs, Sara had grown into her own leader. After spending a few days with Max she saw the same growth in Max. He was becoming physically stronger and believed he could find his family. Sara wanted to lead by example. She felt honored to have been given the opportunity to help Max with finding his way back home to his family.

Strength

Focus

Family

Friendship

Max prepared to leave the ranch. He knew why he had to leave and now he wanted and believed he could accomplish what he set out to do. Together with the help of his new friends he set a daily goal, his strategy for his journey back to where he had come from had been well developed, and he knew how to go about doing what he needed to do. He had a plan. Carlo and Teddy gave him their map. He was set to go back and find his family.

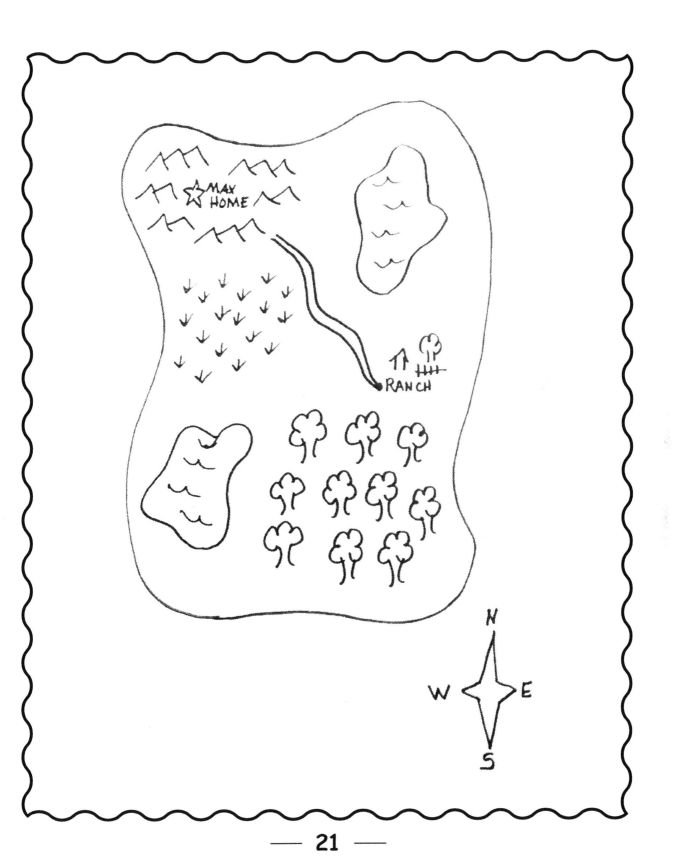

A few months after Max left the ranch Jojo received a letter from Max. She read the letter to everyone at the ranch. Max had found his family.

Max also wrote in the letter how much he appreciated everyone's help. Because it was so helpful to him he asked that you also take a moment each day to write the challenges you are facing today.

For the next 30 days write about a challenge / difficulty / adversity / sad situation <u>you have had</u> to face and how you overcame it. And write about a challenge / difficulty / adversity / sad situation <u>you are facing right now</u> and what you have decided to do to overcome it.

Let your imagination take you anywhere it wants to take you!

Lets begin.

Most importantly - Have fun!

Remember to smile.

Remember to laugh.

Remember to be curious and ask questions.

Remember to Believe in yourself.

Say out loud 10 times.

I Believe in myself.
I Believe in myself.
I Believe in myself.
I Believe in myself.
I Believe in myself.
I Believe in myself.
I Believe in myself.
I Believe in myself.
I Believe in myself.
I Believe in myself.

Day 1

_____

_____

_____

_____

_____

_____

_____

_____

_____

_____

_____

_____

_____

_____

Day 2

_____

_____

_____

_____

_____

_____

_____

_____

_____

_____

_____

_____

Day 3

_____

_____

_____

_____

_____

_____

_____

_____

_____

_____

_____

Day 4

Day 5

_____

_____

_____

_____

_____

_____

_____

_____

_____

_____

_____

_____

_____

Day 6

_____

_____

_____

_____

_____

_____

_____

_____

_____

_____

_____

_____

Day 7

Day 8

_____

_____

_____

_____

_____

_____

_____

_____

_____

_____

_____

_____

Day 9

_____

_____

_____

_____

_____

_____

_____

_____

_____

_____

_____

_____

_____

Day 10

_____

_____

_____

_____

_____

_____

_____

_____

_____

_____

_____

_____

_____

Day 11

_____

_____

_____

_____

_____

_____

_____

_____

_____

_____

_____

_____

_____

Day 12

Day 13

Day 14

Day 15

Day 16

_____

_____

_____

_____

_____

_____

_____

_____

_____

_____

_____

_____

Day 17

_____

_____

_____

_____

_____

_____

_____

_____

_____

_____

_____

_____

Day 18

Day 19

Day 20

_____

_____

_____

_____

_____

_____

_____

_____

_____

_____

_____

_____

Day 21

Day 22

_____

_____

_____

_____

_____

_____

_____

_____

_____

_____

_____

_____

Day 23

Day 24

Day 25

Day 26

_____

_____

_____

_____

_____

_____

_____

_____

_____

_____

_____

_____

Day 27

_____

_____

_____

_____

_____

_____

_____

_____

_____

_____

_____

_____

Day 28

Day 29

Day 30

_____

_____

_____

_____

_____

_____

_____

_____

_____

_____

_____

_____

WOW! YOU ARE AMAZING!!!!!!!!!!!!!!!

YOU DID ALL THE FUN STUFF!

YOU PARTICIPATED IN 30 DAYS OF FUN!

KEEP GOING!

EXPLORE YOUR IMAGINATION!

BELIEVE IN YOURSELF ALWAYS!

SHARE YOUR CHALLENGES, HOW YOU
RESOLVED THEM, AND THE EXPLORATION OF
YOUR IMAGINATION WITH A FRIEND!

THANK YOU FOR BEING GOOD AND
KIND TO EVERY ANIMAL.

On behalf of all the ANIMALS – thank you for
making this a better world for ALL OF US!

Printed in the United States
By Bookmasters